Summer in Antarctica

Written by James Talia

Series Consultant: Linda Hoyt

T0359792

WorldWise™
Content-based Learning

Contents

Introduction

Antarctica is the coldest place on Earth.

For much of the year, it is a dark and icy place. In the middle of winter, there is no sun, it is dark all day and all night, and the seas are frozen.

Strong winds blow across Antarctica for much of the year. Very few animals and plants can live on this cold and windy land.

But this dark and icy place changes for a short time during summer.

April–September

Antarctica

Chapter 1

A melting place

Spring arrives. The sun begins to shine, and there is a little more daylight. As the weather gets warmer, the **sea-ice** starts to **melt**.

Penguins and seals that have spent the winter in warmer seas begin to return to **Antarctica**. Many kinds of whales also make the long journey from warmer waters to Antarctica.

The snow and ice on some parts of the land begin to melt.

October–November

Chapter 2

A summer place

It is summer, and things change quickly in **Antarctica**. The snow and ice keep melting and it is light all day and for most of the night.

During summer, many thousands of animals come out of the sea and move onto the land to have their young. There is plenty of food in the sea now that the ice has melted.

For a very short time, Antarctica becomes a busy and noisy place.

December–January

9

Antarctic food – eating krill

In summer, there are millions of **krill** in the sea around Antarctica.

Krill are like small shrimp. They feed mainly on tiny plants or sometimes on tiny animals that live in Antarctic waters.

Krill are the most important animals in Antarctica, because all the larger animals eat krill, or they feed on animals that eat krill.

Krill

Krill

Penguin

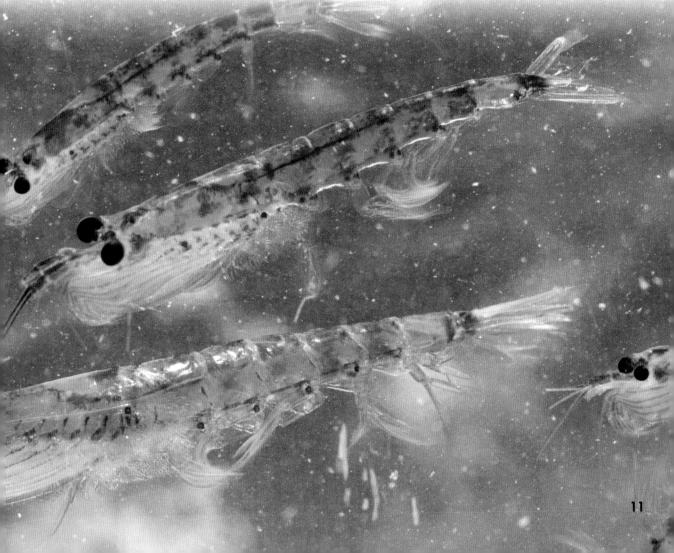

Chapter 3

Penguins and their chicks

Penguins have their young during the short summer.

They make their nests in the same place each year. Some penguins walk up to 56 kilometres over the ice to reach their nesting places. Other penguins walk through deep snow to find a rocky place where they can nest.

Penguins make their nests from small stones. They pick the stones up in their beaks and put them together in the shape of a circle. After the penguins have made their nests, they lay their eggs. Chicks hatch from the eggs.

The parents feed their hungry chicks. The male and female penguins take turns going into the sea to catch food for their young.

The chicks grow very quickly. They need to leave the nest by the end of summer, before the sea begins to **freeze** again. In the autumn, the penguins travel north to warmer weather. They spend the rest of the year at sea.

Find out more

How do penguins stay warm and keep the extremely cold water from freezing their bodies?

Chapter 4

Seals and whales

Seals and their pups

Many different types of seals come to **Antarctica** in summer to have their young. The **pups** are born in late spring and grow quickly during the summer.

The mother seals feed their pups on milk for at least five weeks. After their mother stops feeding them, the pups grow new fur. Soon, they are ready to hunt for their own food.

Find out more

What kinds of seals are found in Antarctica?

Whale visits

Whales visit Antarctica in the summer. This is
when they eat most of their food. Some of them eat
enormous numbers of **krill** — a blue whale can eat up
to four **tonnes** of krill a day! Others hunt penguins and
seals. The whales need to eat lots of food to get ready
for the long journey back to warm waters.

Conclusion

Antarctica is the coldest place on Earth, but summer brings big changes. Many animals come out of the sea to have their young, while some animals travel long distances just to feed there.

Summer in Antarctica is very short. Before long, the weather gets colder, the days get shorter, and the sea starts to **freeze**. The **seabirds** and animals leave with their young on their journeys north.

Antarctica again becomes a dark, quiet and frozen land.

Glossary

Antarctica a large land mass at the most southern part of Earth

freeze to become so cold that water changes from a liquid to a solid

krill small animals that look like shrimp or prawns

melt to change from a solid to a liquid when warmed

pups the young of seals

seabirds birds that spend most of their lives near the sea

sea-ice large areas of ice that form when the sea freezes

tonnes weights equal to 1,000 kilograms

Index